3 1994 01011 1810

SANTA ANA PUBLIC LIBRARY

SANTA ANA
PUBLIC LIBRARY
NEW HOPE

D0821010

Cleopatra

For Sarah

Oxford University Press, 198 Madison Avenue, New York, New York 10016

Oxford   New York
Athens   Auckland   Bangkok   Bogotá   Bombay
Buenos Aires   Calcutta   Cape Town   Dar es Salaam
Delhi   Florence   Hong Kong   Istanbul   Karachi
Kuala Lumpur   Madras   Madrid   Melbourne
Mexico City   Nairobi   Paris   Singapore
Taipei   Tokyo   Toronto   Warsaw

and associated companies in
Berlin   Ibadan

Oxford is a trademark of Oxford University Press

Text © Haydn Middleton 1997
Illustrations © Oxford University Press 1997

Originally published by Oxford University Press UK in 1997.

All rights reserved. No part of this publication may be reproduced, stored in a
retrieval system, or transmitted, in any form or by any means, electronic,
mechanical, photocopying, recording, or otherwise, without the prior
permission of Oxford University Press.

Library of Congress Cataloging-in-Publication Data
Middleton, Haydn.
    Cleopatra / Haydn Middleton : illustrated by Barry Wilkinson.
        p.   cm. – (What's their story?)
    Includes index.
    1. Cleopatra, Queen of Egypt, d. 30 B.C.   2. Egypt –
History – 332–30 B.C.   [1. Cleopatra, Queen of Egypt, d. 30 B.C.
2. Kings, queens, rulers, etc.]   I. Wilkinson, Barry. 1923–   ill.
II. Title.   III. Series.
DT92.7.C54M53   1997
932'.022'092--dc21
[B]   97–27366
                                                                  CIP
                                                                   AC

ISBN 0-19-521404-8

1 3 5 7 9 10 8 6 4 2

Printed in Dubai by Oriental Press

Cleopatra

THE QUEEN OF DREAMS

J B CLEOPATRA MID
Middleton, Haydn
Cleopatra   FEB 0 8 1999

$12.95
BOOKMOBILE 1 31994010111810

HAYDN MIDDLETON

Illustrated by Barry Wilkinson

OXFORD UNIVERSITY PRESS

Two thousand years ago, the king of Egypt had a baby daughter. Her name was Cleopatra. Cleopatra's family had ruled over Egypt for 300 years, but they themselves were not Egyptians. They came from Greece. They spoke Greek, not Egyptian, and they worshiped Greek gods and goddesses.

Cleopatra grew up at her father's court in Alexandria, a rich and beautiful city by the sea. She learned a lot about Egypt's past, when the pyramids had been built and the kings were called pharaohs.

She found out that the pharaohs had once ruled over many lands in Asia and Africa, as well as Egypt. All these lands had formed a huge Egyptian Empire. Cleopatra wished that Egypt still had an empire stretching far and wide. It was so much grander to rule an empire than just a kingdom.

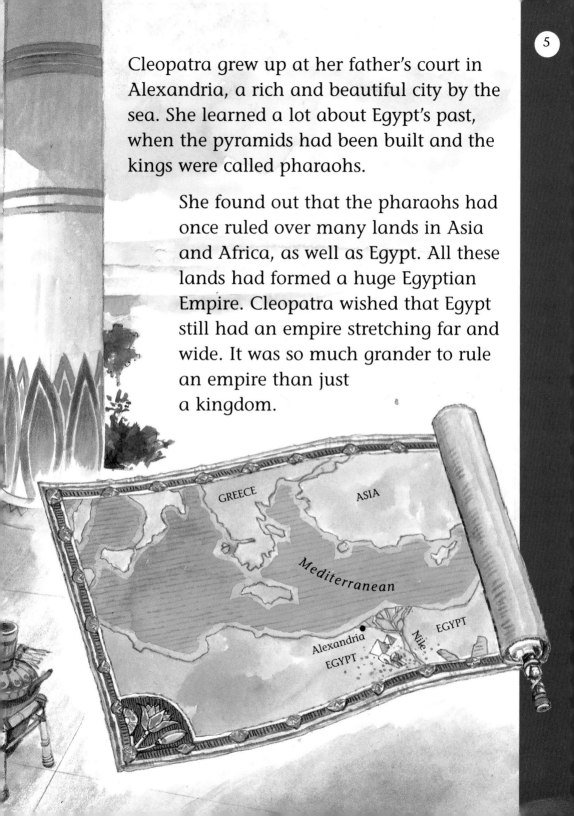

Cleopatra was 18 when her father died. Her brother now had to rule Egypt. The new king's name was Ptolemy. He was only 10 years old, but already he was married. It happened like this.

The Egyptians had a goddess named Isis, who was married to her brother Osiris. Brothers and sisters in the Egyptian royal family used to marry each other too. So little King Ptolemy's wife was . . . his sister Cleopatra!

When Cleopatra became queen she was a well-educated young woman. She could speak several languages, including Egyptian, and her voice was especially beautiful. People loved to be with her, just to hear her speak. But her brother and his advisers ignored her. They thought that only men knew how to rule.

Cleopatra was determined that one day she would prove them wrong.

Egypt was a rich country, but life was hard for many of its people. They prayed to a number of gods for help, like Ra, the king of the sun. They sometimes worshiped their rulers, too. Cleopatra became very popular with the ordinary people of Egypt. They called her the daughter of Ra.

Cleopatra liked being worshiped in this way. She also enjoyed seeing statues of herself looking like the goddess Isis. Egypt's religion became very important to her. She took part in holy processions and paid for old ruined temples to be rebuilt.

Some Eastern holy books said that one day a mysterious woman would rule first Egypt and then "the whole wide world." Cleopatra hoped it would be her. But King Ptolemy had other plans for his sister. Even though the people were starting to love Cleopatra, he and his advisers chased her out of Egypt. This was partly because she was planning to make the Egyptians friendlier with the mighty Romans.

Agreat Roman leader arrived in Alexandria. He had once lent money to Cleopatra's father. Now he wanted to be paid back. His name was Julius Caesar, and he had led the Roman army to many victories. Some people said he would soon become king in Rome. This would have been unusual. For hundreds of years there had been no Roman royal family. Instead, Rome's leading citizens had regular "elections," when they chose who would rule them.

Caesar heard that Ptolemy and Cleopatra had argued.
So he invited both of them to come to him and try to
make up.

Ptolemy came, but his advisers put guards around
Caesar's palace to stop Cleopatra from getting in, too.
Cleopatra would not be put off. She hid herself inside a
rug. The rug was sent as a present to Caesar, and when
he unrolled it inside his palace, out jumped the queen!

Ptolemy refused to rule with Cleopatra. So Caesar led the Romans in a war against him and put Cleopatra back on her throne. Ptolemy died in the fighting, so Cleopatra's younger brother became her husband. But the man she lived with now was Julius Caesar himself.

Caesar was 52 years old, and Cleopatra was just 20. After a short stay with Cleopatra in Egypt, Caesar returned to Rome. Cleopatra went to join him. There they made plans for the Egyptians and Romans to work closely together in the future.

Cleopatra hoped that the Romans could help her to conquer a new Egyptian Empire. But Caesar had enemies in Rome. They thought he had become too powerful, so they murdered him. Cleopatra fled back to Egypt, taking her young son, Caesarion, with her.

After Caesar died, several men tried to rule Rome together. One was Caesar's clever young adopted son, Octavian. Another was a brave and handsome soldier named Mark Antony. These two men never really trusted each other, but in the end they made an agreement. The Romans had conquered many lands in Europe, Africa, and Asia. Octavian took charge of all the western lands, and Antony took the east.

Before his death, Caesar had been planning to invade the mighty Parthian Empire, which spread right across our modern-day countries of Iraq and Iran. Antony decided to put these plans into action and win everlasting fame. But he needed someone to help him to pay his armies. He knew the queen of Egypt was rich, so he sent her messages to come and talk with him at Tarsus.

Cleopatra also needed Antony's help. He might just be able to make her dream of a new Egyptian Empire come true. So she came to Tarsus dressed as Venus, the Roman goddess of love, on a barge so gorgeous that it took everyone's breath away. She hoped to win Antony's heart, just as she had won Caesar's.

Antony soon fell under Cleopatra's spell. But she fell under his, too. In many ways they were like each other. They both loved to enjoy life, and both had grand dreams for the future.

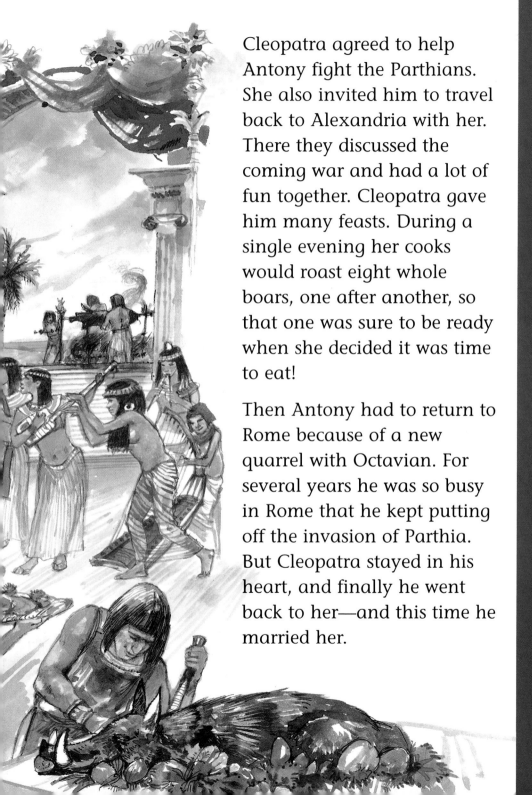

Cleopatra agreed to help Antony fight the Parthians. She also invited him to travel back to Alexandria with her. There they discussed the coming war and had a lot of fun together. Cleopatra gave him many feasts. During a single evening her cooks would roast eight whole boars, one after another, so that one was sure to be ready when she decided it was time to eat!

Then Antony had to return to Rome because of a new quarrel with Octavian. For several years he was so busy in Rome that he kept putting off the invasion of Parthia. But Cleopatra stayed in his heart, and finally he went back to her—and this time he married her.

Antony and Cleopatra had three children. They named the first two after the Greek gods of the sun and the moon, Helios and Selene. Antony was just as interested in religion as Cleopatra was. He said that Dionysus, a Greek god similar to Egyptian Osiris, was his special protector. Dionysus was a god of wine and dancing. His worshipers held wild, drunken processions in his honor.

Antony liked to think that he was a kind of human god himself. If Cleopatra was the new Isis, then he was the new Dionysus. He believed that together they could start a Golden Age, when East and West would live in perfect peace.

But first there was a war to fight. At last Antony was ready to attack Parthia. He marched east at the head of a vast army. His hopes were high. As soon as he had beaten the Parthians, he planned to lead his men against Octavian. Then he would prove to everyone that he was Rome's true master.

Antony knew the Parthians would be hard to beat. Few Romans had won victories against them before. Their empire was large, and their archers were especially deadly in battle. In the end, the Parthians proved too much for Antony's army.

The Romans could not break down the walls of the cities on their route. They lost many soldiers in surprise attacks by the Parthians. They won some battles, but soon they were fighting against hunger, thirst, and disease as well. Antony saw that they could not win. Grimly he led his surviving men back.

But Cleopatra raised his spirits. She made him remember all their old dreams for the future. Now they decided to tell the world about those dreams.

The people of Alexandria had never seen anything like it. Cleopatra and Antony were giving the biggest party ever. Huge crowds flocked to the city's great athletics stadium. That was where the "Donations" ceremony was held.

On a stage made of silver, on thrones made of gold, Antony and Cleopatra sat dressed as Dionysus and Isis. On smaller thrones sat their own three children, and also young Caesarion. Antony introduced Caesarion as the son of Julius Caesar, and named him King of Kings. Then he named Cleopatra Queen of Kings. The other children were called rulers too. They all wore the costumes of the countries that one day they would rule over.

Some of these countries had not yet been conquered, but others belonged to Rome. When Octavian heard about Antony's Donations—or gifts of land—he was furious. He knew that Cleopatra had always wanted an empire for Egypt. But he would not let her simply take it from Rome.

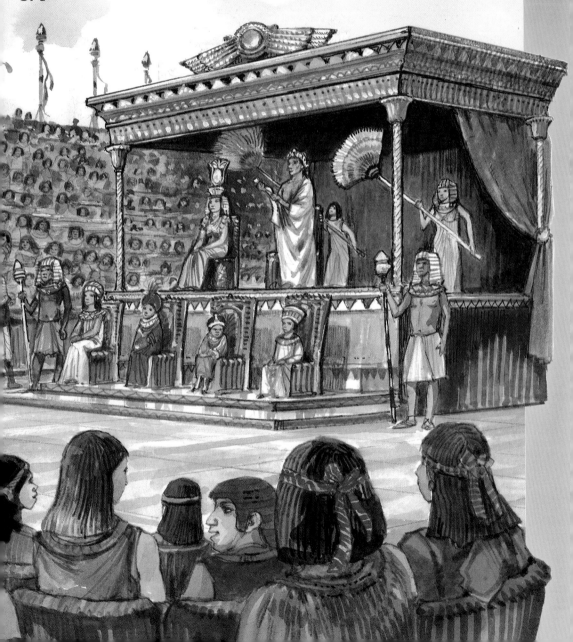

For years Octavian and Antony had been heading for a huge fight. They had never liked each other. Octavian disliked Cleopatra, too. He blamed her for making Antony more like an Egyptian than a Roman. At last he declared war on her. That meant he was declaring war on Antony, too.

Octavian's supporters came to him in Greece. Many more men joined Antony at Ephesus in Asia. Cleopatra brought huge amounts of treasure to pay them. She and Antony held great religious festivals, to make sure that the gods were on their side as well. Then they moved on to Actium, where things began to go wrong.

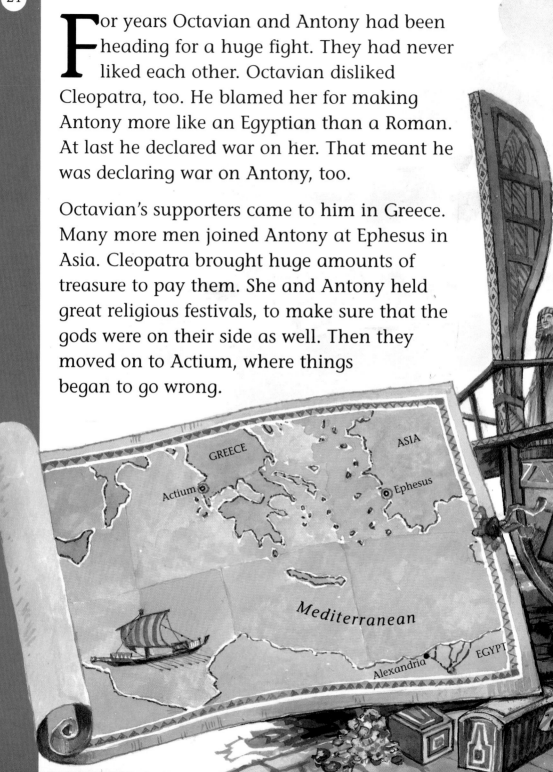

Octavian managed to surround their camp by the sea.
Some of Antony's followers panicked and changed sides.
Antony had wanted a land battle. Now he had to lead
out his navy to fight Octavian at sea.

Around noon on a day in early September, the Battle of Actium began. It was over almost at once. Antony's navy left the harbor. Cleopatra's Egyptian ships, with all her treasure, were at the back. Then suddenly Cleopatra's ships headed away toward Egypt—and Antony hurried after her in a ship of his own. Maybe they were escaping so that they could fight Octavian later, on land. But Antony's men did not know that. Amazed and confused, they surrendered.

Cleopatra and Antony made it back to Egypt. But Octavian had not finished yet. His armies closed in on Alexandria and beat its defenders in another battle. He had won the war. Soon he would become the first Roman emperor, and call himself Augustus. But what would happen to Antony and Cleopatra?

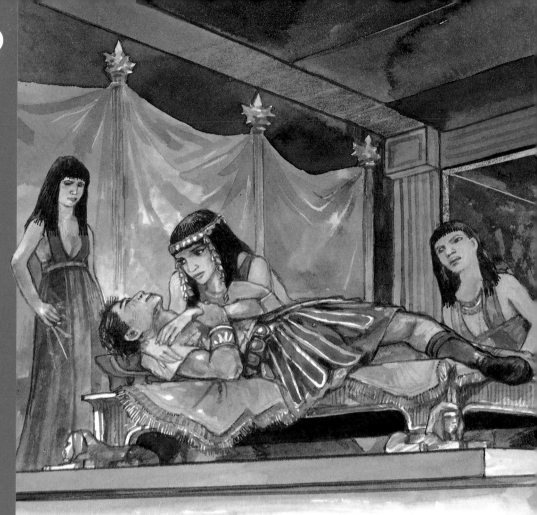

Cleopatra had earlier built a kind of tomb for herself. It was like a little fortress, with room inside for all her treasure. Before the last battle she hid there, to be safe with her servants.

Meanwhile, Antony had lost all hope. Ghostly noises filled the streets at night, loud at first, then growing softer. People said it was the god Dionysus, Antony's old protector, dancing out of Alexandria. Antony felt so alone. Then even worse news came: Cleopatra was dead.

In despair Antony stabbed himself, and began to die, too. Then different news arrived. His wife was still alive! She ordered two slaves to bring him to her great tomb. But it was too late to save him. Bleeding, he died in Cleopatra's arms. Then Octavian's men burst in and took the queen prisoner.

Octavian let Cleopatra give Antony a fine funeral. She wept for her dead husband, but also for herself. She knew that now Octavian would take her to Rome. He would lead her through the streets in chains. Roman crowds would laugh and spit at her. Anything, she thought, would be better than that.

At her last meal, she ordered a basket of figs. People said afterward that she arranged for a snake to be hidden among them. The snake, an asp, was holy to Ra, the sun god. It was also highly poisonous. Octavian's officers came in later to find Cleopatra lying dead in her robes of Isis. There was a tiny bite mark on her arm. She was 39 years old.

The queen of dreams was buried with Antony. All their grand plans had come to nothing. Now, side by side, the two of them could dream forever.

Important dates in Cleopatra's life

Index